THEOLOGY
OF THE BODY
for Teens

HIGH SCHOOL EDITION

Parent's Guide

Jason Evert

ASCENSION
PRESS
West Chester, Pennsylvania

Ascension Press
Post Office Box 1990
West Chester, PA 19380
Customer Service: 1-800-376-0520
AscensionPress.com
TOBforTeens.com

Cover design: Devin Schadt

Printed in the United States of America
12 13 8 7 6 5 4

ISBN 978-1-934217-38-2

CONTENTS

INTRODUCTION

There is only one kind of person who dislikes having to do homework more than a teenager … and that's the *parent* of a teenager. As a father of three young children—who are all currently in diapers—I understand the value of a moment of free time. For that reason, I thank you for picking up this booklet and reading this far. I hope that you will find it to be a worthwhile investment of your free time.

As the primary educator of your children, you have the right to know what material will be presented to your son or daughter through our high school curriculum *Theology of the Body for Teens*. The purpose of this booklet is to offer you a brief overview of the topics to be discussed with your student and suggestions for making the material come alive at home.

When it comes to the topic of human sexuality, some parents have given their teenagers numerous talks on chastity. Others are terrified to even mention the subject. Regardless of where you fall on the spectrum, we hope this booklet will empower you to communicate effectively with your teen. Research shows that the majority of adults (91 percent) and teens (87 percent) think that it would be easier for teens to be abstinent if they could discuss the topic of sexuality with their parents. However nearly 40 percent of teens say they have not had a single conversation about the issue with their parents![1] The bottom line is simple: if you do not speak to your teens about the meaning of human sexuality and love, the world will fill the void of your silence with a very contrary message.

They *Are* Listening To You

No parent is unaware of the constant IV drip of indulgence, instant gratification, and lust that pours into the minds of teenagers through the noise of iPods, the Internet, and television. It is enough to make some parents feel immobilized, as if they have no chance to compete. In fact, the average high school student watches more than twenty-one hours of TV per week and listens to three to four hours of music per day! That's more time than a teen will spend in the classroom.

That said, we parents have more influence than we might initially believe. Even if our teen is simultaneously text-messaging a friend while watching TV, listening to his iPod, doing homework, and rolling his eyes at you, his heart is open. He's just multi-tasking. The noise of the world will never drown out the love you express to him on a daily basis. Although young people often act as if they want to be left alone, they are actually pining for interference from dad and mom. They are searching for love and meaning in their lives. It is for these very reasons that we have designed this curriculum.

Because young people seem to have a limitless appetite for idealism and love, they must be offered a guide that will help them fulfill these noble desires. Blessed John Paul II's Theology of the Body explains that the road map to discover one's purpose in life is closer than we might imagine.

The Theology of the Body Isn't Just for Teens

As you read through these pages, open your heart to the ways in which these teachings might impact your own relationships and family life. The Theology of the Body is meant for every person, regardless of one's age or marital status.

All too often, the Church's moral laws are seen as arbitrary rules passed down from officials in the Vatican. Many people experience these teachings as external and even imposed. The beauty of John Paul II's

Theology of the Body, though, is that it presents the Church's teaching on human sexuality as if it were coming from within our own hearts.

Although the idea of teaching theology to your teenager may seem intimidating, you don't need to have any religious education experience to communicate these truths to your son or daughter. To the degree you love, you will be able to make this curriculum come to life for your high school student. In fact, nothing teaches a child to love as eloquently as a parent who loves unconditionally. As the saying goes, "Although your children may not always obey you, they will never fail to imitate you."

Some parents hesitate to speak to their teen about chastity out of fear that he or she will ask probing personal questions such as, "Well, were you a virgin when you got married?" While some parents may have no reason to fear such an interrogation, many have allowed their pasts to paralyze them. What you as a parent must realize is that the source of your authority does not come from your perfection—or lack thereof. It comes from the fact that you are the parent. If you have made mistakes in the past, and you have repented of them, you have nothing to fear. You can use those experiences to teach your teen to make better decisions. Either way, parents must overcome their insecurities when it comes to talking to their teenagers about chastity. For their sakes, we cannot afford to be silent.

Created for Love

Can you imagine a world in which there was no divorce, sexual abuse, depression, sexually-transmitted diseases, eating disorders, addictions, cheating, or unwed pregnancies?

It seems unimaginable, doesn't it? But if we all long for such a world, why do we live in such a different one? If we were made for love, why does it seem that authentic love is so hard to find? And if we want love, why do we so often settle for its counterfeits? The twelve chapters in the *Theology of the Body for Teens* curriculum set out to answer these questions for your teenager.

In the first chapter, "Created for Love," we set out to open the minds and hearts of the students to the fact that God, who is love, created them out of love and calls them to love. To explore this subject, we delve into the following points:

- God designed us for union with Him and with others.

- Our bodies have been created by God and are good.

- Our bodies reveal deep truths about the meaning of life.

- Through our bodies, we make visible the love of God.

Learning and Experiencing the Love We Deserve

These topics are profound, but the aim of this curriculum is not mere intellectual knowledge. Rather, the purpose of this program is to urge our teenagers to examine their lives by looking at their deepest yearning, the need for love. God placed this desire within all of us so that it would actually lead us back to Him.

Unfortunately, because of the effects of original sin, love is often confused with lust, which is the selfish desire to *use* another person. While original sin may sound like a foggy theological concept, teens easily grasp the "fall of man" when they consider its effects. Some teens have shared:

- "I hooked up with him because I thought it would make him like me more. But the next day, he acted like he hardly knew me."

- "My parents got divorced when I was four, so I never really had a dad. Now my mom is with this other guy, but they fight a lot."

- "I've been hooked on pornography for years and I don't know how to stop looking at the stuff."

- "No one has ever seemed interested in me. I hate my body."

- "You always hear about the guys using the girls, but after I gave my virginity to my girlfriend, I found out she was cheating on me."

> *"Man cannot live without love. He remains a being that is incomprehensible for himself, his life is senseless, if love is not revealed to him, if he does not encounter love, if he does not experience it and make it his own, if he does not intimately participate in it."*
>
> - *Blessed John Paul II*

Such tragic testimonies are more common in the lives of teenagers than most adults would like to admit. The fact is, though, that most high school students have struggled in at least one of these areas. But no matter how wounded or innocent a teenager may be, deep within the heart of every one of them is the desire for a love that is true, good, and beautiful. Unfortunately, because of the influence of media and the modern culture, many teens feel lost at sea when it comes to finding love and meaning in their lives. I have found that when Catholics—young and old alike—find out that such confusion and pain was not how it was "in the beginning," they begin to have hope that answers to their heart's longings are possible.

> *"Life is not worth living unless it is lived for others."*
>
> *- Blessed Teresa of Calcutta*

"In the Beginning, It Was Not So"

When God created us, He made us in His image and likeness. We may have heard that phrase of Jesus ("In the beginning, it was not so") often but may have not considered what it really means for our lives. The Bible says "God is love" (1 Jn 4:8). When love is present, it is never in isolation. This is why a person cannot marry himself. Rather, love requires three things: a lover, a beloved, and the love between them. There must be a communion of persons, united in love. So, in the case of God, we have the Father, the Son, and the fire of love between them, the Holy Spirit.

In making us male and female, God designed us to reflect his life-giving love by becoming a sincere gift to one another. Especially through the union of spouses in marriage, a husband and wife make visible to the world the invisible reality of God—that He is love. But no matter what a person's state in life (married, single, or religious), everyone is able to make a gift of himself or herself. For this reason, Blessed John Paul II recalled the words of Vatican II, which said, "Man can fully discover his true self only in a sincere gift of self."[2]

This calling to make a gift of ourselves is stamped into our bodies. In our complementarity as male and female, God has stamped into our design a call to give ourselves to another. A man's body does not make sense by itself, nor does a woman's body. They make sense in light of the other. This is a key concept that underpins Blessed John Paul II's landmark work known as the Theology of the Body. Simply put, the body is a key to understanding the very meaning of our lives.

 Questions for Your Teen

1. How can I love you better?

2. How can you love others in your life in an authentic way?

3. Do you believe that God loves you?

4. What do you think of the idea that the male body only makes sense in light of a woman's body?

1. For every child, the love of God is first made visible through the love of a father and mother. When a child's parents are generous, merciful, patient, affectionate, and present, that child or teenager will be much more able to conceive of a God who possesses the same attributes.

2. The best thing a husband can do for his children is to love his wife. The same could be said of the wife loving her husband. A teenager may read about love in this curriculum, but the true school of love is the family. A teenage girl once said to me that the example of her father sets the standard for all other guys. One night he said to her, "Maggie, I hope one day you'll find a man that loves you as much as I love your mother." Understandably, this made quite an impression on her. Even if you are raising your son or daughter without the other parent, you are sharing a life-giving love with your children through the sacrifices you make for them on a daily basis.

3. The nature of God as a loving union of persons is much easier to grasp when one's own family resembles this. What things could be done within your family to deepen the unity between its members? Perhaps it means turning the TV off during dinner or praying more often as a family. Whatever the case may be, do not be afraid to introduce new traditions in your family that will strengthen its bond for years to come.

Love Defined:
Giving versus Using

In the first chapter, we invite teens to consider that they have been created for love. Such a concept is easily grasped by the young, who long for acceptance and affirmation. No teen doubts that his or her deepest desire is love.

Confusion arises, however, when it comes to the meaning of love. When a high school student meets with friends at the movie theater, it will only be a matter of time before a "love" story unfolds before them on the screen. Unfortunately, such portrayals of love usually amount to nothing more than infatuation, lust, or both.

While a parent may want to counteract such negative messages, how can anyone compete with multimillion dollar movies, countless commercials, pop-up ads, and airbrushed billboards? The same teenager who listens to hours of music a day on his iPod seems to have a six-second attention span when his parents are talking to him. How do we break through?

The Power of Love

Only one thing is powerful enough to expose the counterfeits of love … and that is love itself. The National Campaign to Prevent Teen Pregnancy surveyed teenagers, asking them to identify the number one factor that shapes the decisions they make about their sexuality.[3] Was it their peers? Their music? Their siblings? Parents suspected that it was the friends. However, according to the teenagers themselves, the most influential thing that affected the decisions they made regarding sexuality was their parents. Therefore, do not underestimate your ability to reach your teen.

In *Theology of the Body for Teens*, we set out to remind the teenagers of the essence of true love. Thankfully, God has already stamped a desire for it within them. Our job is to remind them of what they already know.

So, what is love? Perhaps Blessed John Paul II defined it best when he wrote, "For love is not merely a feeling; it is an act of the will that consists of preferring, in a constant manner, the good of others to the good of one's self."[4] Teens can perceive the difference between this kind of love, and its counterfeit, which is lust. Whereas love is self-giving, lust involves using another for one's own pleasure.

While emotion, desire, and attraction all play a role in love, they are all too often confused with love itself. Teens often believe that the stronger their

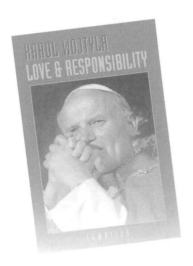

emotions are towards another, the more real love there is. However, Blessed John Paul II clarifies the matter for us, saying, "The greater the feeling of responsibility for the person the more true love there is."[5]

Once a person understands the meaning of love, he or she can apply that information in his or her relationships. By doing so, the concept of chastity begins to make sense.

Redeeming Chastity

Usually when teens hear the term "chastity," what comes to their minds? Odds are it is the word "NO!" Here is how your son or daughter might imagine a typical conversation between a student and a religion teacher.

Student: Is it OK for my girlfriend and me to …

Teacher: NO.

Student: Well, what if we just …

Teacher: NO.

Student: But what if we really …

Teacher: NO. NO. NO. Just don't. Be good boys and girls. Hold hands and go to a pumpkin patch together, then play board games with her family, and be home by 7:00 p.m. Otherwise you'll get her pregnant and die of an STD. Class dismissed. Have a fun weekend!

While this is *not* a fair picture of religion teachers, it *is* a fair representation of the way many teens *view* the concept of chastity. With such negative ideas associated with the word, it is understandable why Blessed John Paul II said that the word "chastity" needs to be rehabilitated.

If people understood the true purpose of chastity, they would see that it has nothing to do with fear or prudishness. Nor is it a repression of sexual desires. Rather, chastity is an exercise of the will to choose what is good. It is a refusal to allow the desire for pleasure to displace the call to love. Pleasure is not a bad thing, but when a person pursues enjoyment at the expense of another, love is abandoned.

This is why John Paul II tells us that chastity can only be thought of in association with love. When love is present, the man and woman have

> "Now is the time to begin to prepare yourself for family life. You cannot fulfill this path if you do not know how to love. To love means to want to perfect yourself and your beloved, to overcome your selfishness, and give yourself completely."
>
> - St. Gianna Molla

a sincere desire to do what is good for the other. Therefore, when it comes to teenage dating relationships, chastity frees the couple from using each other as objects, and thus makes them capable of authentic love.

When lust takes precedence over love, pleasure becomes one's goal and the other person becomes only a means to it. To such a person, chastity is seen as an obstacle. It serves no purpose but to threaten his or her lifestyle. But we should not be afraid of the demands of love. If teens can see the beauty of God's plan for human love, they will desire it. They will not choose His ways out of fear of pregnancy or STDs, but rather because God's plan for love is everything that the human heart longs for.

Within every person is a battle between love and lust. As one husband said, "Winning this battle takes faith in Christ, dedication, commitment, honesty with ourselves and others, and a willingness to make sacrifices and deny our own selfish desires. But love is not afraid of those things; love is those things."[6] Once we understand this, we will be able to understand why Blessed John Paul II said that "only the chaste man and the chaste woman are capable of true love."[7]

Questions for Your Teen

1. What was the last movie you saw that portrayed true, sacrificial love?

2. What do most of your classmates think love is?

3. What do you think is the meaning of love?

4. Does the idea of living a chaste life challenge you, interest you, scare you?

1. Consider ways that you can teach your teenager the meaning of love without using words. For example, through listening well, practicing small acts of thoughtfulness, attending sports games, etc. Don't be discouraged if your teen fails to notice your efforts. The cumulative force of years of love will have a lasting impact.

2. Tell your son or daughter that you love them (daily).

3. Be affectionate to your teens, even if they squirm. The value of a simple human touch is too easily forgotten. In fact, teens today are starved for affection, and they often seek out physical relationships in order to meet their emotional needs. By being affectionate to them, you provide a small antidote to counteract the allure of empty physical relationships.

4. Persevere in the virtue of love at home. When a teen witnesses his parents practicing years of patience, tenderness, and faithfulness, a teen will easily grasp the meaning of love. Lust and infatuation will be seen for what they are: counterfeits.

5. Consider the practice of pointing out images of "love" and "lust" that appear in everyday media that accidentally interrupt your family life.

Naked Without Shame

When using an online mapping website, the first piece of information required is your starting point. Without knowing this, it would be impossible for the computer to create directions toward your destination. In the same way, in order for your teenagers to understand themselves, they must understand God's original plan in creating them.

In chapter three of *Theology of the Body for Teens*, we unpack the following topics:

- God created man and woman in His image and likeness.

- God is love, and His call for us to love is stamped into our bodies.

- In the beginning, the innocence of Adam and Eve allowed them to be "naked without shame."

- With the fall of man, lust and shame entered the picture.

- Original sin still affects our daily lives, but there is hope.

When most teenagers think about the story of Adam and Eve, they often recollect only three things: a talking snake, an apple, and a naked couple wearing plants. As a result, our teens often give the biblical accounts of creation about as much credibility as Alice in Wonderland or the Easter Bunny.

The Power of a Pure Heart

A deeper look at authentic purity shows that Christ came to redeem mankind from our fall:

> In the early Christian Church, several bishops were gathered outside a cathedral in Antioch, when a beautiful prostitute passed by on the street. Upon noticing her, the crowd of bishops looked away to avoid being seduced. Bishop Nonnus, however, stared intently at her, and then said to his fellow bishops, "Did not the wonderful beauty of that woman delight you?" The bishops remained silent. Nonnus insisted, "Indeed it delighted me," but he wept for her. When the prostitute saw how the bishop looked at her, she was caught off guard. No man had ever looked at her with such purity. He was not lusting after her, but rather saw something in her that she did not even see in herself. The simple purity of that one bishop's glance marked the beginning of her conversion to Christ. She soon returned to seek his spiritual guidance, and today, we know this former prostitute as St. Pelagia.

Bishop Nonnus was not afraid that the sight of her body would force him to lust. Rather, her body revealed his call to love her properly. He didn't see a prostitute walking toward him—he saw a woman, made in the image and likeness of God. Though he lived many centuries before Blessed John Paul II, he truly lived out the future pope's words when he said that God "assigns the dignity of every woman as a task to every man."[8]

While we need to practice custody of the eyes and avoid occasions of sin, God ultimately wants to transform our hearts so that we aren't afraid we will lust every time we see an attractive person. This is the freedom exhibited by Bishop Nonnus and offered to all of us. Similarly, God offered St. Pelagia freedom and gave her the grace to help her grow out of the habit of allowing herself to be used. No matter how old we are, where we have been, or what we've done, purity is possible! It may seem difficult to attain, but all things are possible with God (Luke 1:37).

The "Spousal Meaning" of the Body

While the story of Bishop Nonnus and St. Pelagia should inspire us towards the goal of Christian purity, it also reveals something of our origin. In the beginning, God created man and woman in his image and likeness. Adam and Eve were naked, and yet they experienced no shame. How was it that Adam could look upon the body of Eve, and not lust?

At the dawn of creation, everything was pure, including the heart of man. For example, Adam experienced sexual desire in a totally pure way. When Adam first saw Eve, he saw her as God intended for her to be seen. There wasn't any confusion between love and lust. When he saw her body, he didn't want to use her. He saw and experienced his call to love her. This may be hard to imagine because many teenagers (and adults) have been led to believe that sex itself is bad or "dirty." But when God originally designed us, sexual desire was the desire to love in the image of God. In other words, sexual desire was a pure desire to give to the other. Sexual desire was an expression of the person who desired to make a gift of self (a self-donation) to another person. According to Blessed John Paul II, their innocence allowed Adam and Eve to be naked without shame.

Because of the purity of their hearts, Adam and Eve's naked bodies revealed their call to make a gift of themselves to each other. This is what Blessed John Paul II called the "spousal meaning of the body." In the physical design of their

> *"True love is a love in which sexual values are subordinate to the value of the person."*
>
> *-Blessed John Paul II*

bodies, Adam and Eve saw that their bodies literally fit together; they knew they were made for a communion that is sacred. This is what the "spousal meaning" means. God made them as a gift for each other. By giving themselves to one another, Adam and Eve were able to mirror the very life of God. The Trinity is a communion of persons, a family of love. So, too, is an earthly family a communion of love.

Unfortunately, with the fall of Adam and Eve, this original innocence was lost. They realized that they were naked, and their original state of innocence was shattered. Shame entered the picture. Although some people would like to think that original sin is simply a quaint religious idea, its effects are hard to dispute.

The Effects of Shame

Adam and Eve did not trust God's plan for them, and this same attitude of prideful distrust is alive and well today. In our curriculum, we ask your teenagers to consider for themselves:

- How often do we doubt the goodness of God and feel the need to break away from Him in order to satisfy our desires?

- How often do we want to decide what is right instead of trusting God and following His ways?

- How often do we grasp at what feels like love, only to discover that it was a counterfeit? We're left with regrets, and we may even come to doubt that love is possible.

Because of original sin, mankind forgets the goodness of the body. Sadly, many people today even harbor a sense of hatred for their own bodies. Eating disorders, cutting, and even steroid use are often symptoms of self-loathing. Because we are bombarded by a culture that expects every man to have six-pack abs and every girl to wear a size zero, many of our teens (if not most) feel inadequate.

While some people are ashamed of their bodies, others deal with shame by becoming shameless. In other words, they learn to feel no remorse for their desire to use another person, or to be used themselves. They make no effort to overcome this selfish urge with selfless love. This usually happens because they have numbed their consciences.

> *"Shame is a tendency, uniquely characteristic of the human person, to conceal sexual values sufficiently to preserve them from obscuring the value of the person as such."*
>
> *- Blessed John Paul II*

The Hope of Redemption

However, original sin has not annihilated our ability to love. Blessed John Paul II tells us that only true love is capable of absorbing shame. This means that shame is "swallowed up by love, dissolved in it, so that the man and woman are no longer ashamed" of sharing themselves and their sexuality with each other.[9] When a husband and wife understand each other's value as persons, they are safe. There should be no shame because they are making a total gift of themselves in life-giving love. After all, what could be shameful about loving as God loves?

Because of the redemption that is offered to us in Christ, our hearts can be renewed. Because Christ's death on the cross won for us the grace not only to be saved, but also to transform our fallen inclinations, a husband and wife can again experience something of that original nakedness without shame. They

"Jesus came to restore creation to the purity if its origins."

- CCC 2336

can experience the authentic, safe, self-donating love that we are all seeking.

Questions for Your Teen

1. Does the way a girl dresses affect the way men treat her?

2. Why do you think fashions have become more immodest over time?

3. If most girls want to find a guy who knows how to treat her like a lady, why do you think that so many girls dress immodestly?

4. Do you think that teenage guys appreciate the real value of women?

5. What do you think it means to "trust God"?

6. Do you trust God?

1. When God created man and woman, he said that they were "very good." Many teens today are starved for affirmation, and they make poor relationship decisions when flattered by a member of the opposite sex. To help your children (and spouse) know their value, praise them at least twice for every time you offer advice or criticism.

2. Most modern fashions are shameless. In order to restore Christian modesty, do not be afraid to tell your daughter, "You are not leaving this house in that outfit!" Use it as an opportunity to explain how immodest attire distracts men from seeing her real value.

3. Many young women feel unable to compete with the starving models depicted in teen magazines. Many young men expect women to live up to such an unhealthy standard. In order to create an environment free of such unrealistic expectations, review your son or daughter's magazines and remove anything that does not belong in a Christian home. Although your teenager might claim "first amendment rights" or protest against such an "exercise of unconstitutional censorship," stand firm in your resolve to maintain a pure home. It will also be helpful to use this as a teaching moment, giving some sort of explanation in the process. This sends a message that you are not being unreasonable and also that Christianity has a strong response to the moral issues we face in the modern culture.

Hope and
Redemption in Christ

While they often appear stoic and independent, many teenagers today carry hidden emotional wounds that weigh down their hearts. Despite the fact that the media portrays teen sex without regrets, a survey of 1,000 sexually active teens across America revealed that two-thirds of them wish that they had waited longer to have sex (77 percent of girls and 60 percent of boys).[10]

If your teen has made poor decisions when it comes to his or her sexuality, do not blame yourself. After all, who is the best parent in the universe? It is the Heavenly Father. Now look at how messed up most of His kids are, here on earth! It's not because he is a defective dad. It's because his children have the gift of free wills, and they do not always use it wisely.

Because the gift of sexuality is so often misused, many young people struggle with:

- Self-hatred
- Guilt
- Memories of abuse
- Insecurity
- Sexual addictions

No matter what may be weighing on a person's heart, God is able to bring healing and restoration. In our fourth chapter, "Hope and Redemption in Christ," we introduce the students to the boundless mercy of God.

We discuss with your teen the fact that when we return to God, He not only forgives their sins, He offers them a new heart. Christ did not die and rise from the dead so that they could repress their sexuality and simply "try their best not to think about sex." He did not come to simply redeem their souls and then leave them with a bunch of coping mechanisms to battle temptation. Thankfully, He came to redeem every part of them, including their bodies and their desires.

Christ came to offer everyone victory and freedom. Sadly, instead of claiming this victory, teenagers often complain that purity is too difficult. By doing this, they empty the Cross of its power and meaning. They reduce redemption to some quaint religious idea that sounds good but has no real power to change them. By doing so, they fail to experience its life-changing effects.

Becoming a New Creation

So what does a teenager need to do? First, he or she must realize that purity is a gift from God and that He will give it to those who ask for it. The ideal place to seek the gift of purity

> *"Our sins are nothing but a grain of sand alongside the great mountain of the mercy of God."*
>
> -St. John Vianney

> *"As far as the east is from the west, so far does he remove our transgressions from us."*
>
> *- Psalm 103:12*

is in the sacrament of Reconciliation. Jesus promised us that He would be with us until the end, and one of the ways He is present to us right now is in the sacraments of the Church.

Teenagers and adults alike may avoid confession, out of fear or embarrassment. Some act as if the sacrament is irrelevant, thinking, "Well, I can just go straight to God when I need forgiveness." But by having this mentality, many people miss out on the extraordinary graces waiting for them in Confession. In the words of St. Augustine, "I would be hiding You from myself, not myself from You."

Jesus instituted the sacrament of Reconciliation because He knew we need it (John 20:21-23). To cast it aside would be like a child disregarding the wishes of his mother, and throwing off a life preserver. Just as a stubborn child overestimates his independence, so too do many people exercise a spiritual independence from the Church. What is needed is humility. In the words of Blessed John Paul II, "In order to see Jesus, we first need to let Him look at us!"[11]

Through confession, we are made new. However, Jesus did not come to earth simply to redeem our souls. Perhaps one of the most ignored teachings of Christianity is that Christ also came to redeem our bodies. When we die, our bodies and souls will be separated, but only for a while. At the resurrection of the dead, those who are saved will receive glorified bodies. This is why the *Catechism* states, "'On no point does the Christian faith meet with more opposition than on the resurrection of the body.' It is very commonly accepted that the life of the human person continues in a spiritual fashion after death. But how can we believe that this body, so clearly mortal, could rise to everlasting life?" (CCC 996).

> *"Have patience with all the world, but first of all with yourself."*
>
> -*St. Francis De Sales*

Earlier in our curriculum, we pointed out that our bodies reveal our call to make a gift of ourselves in love, the spousal meaning of the body. However, the giving of our bodies to another person in marriage is only part of God's plan. Just as our bodies point us to an earthly union with a spouse, they also point us to the eternal union with God in heaven. This is why the Bible states that heaven is the consummation of marriage between Christ and the Church.

Questions for Your Teen

1. How do you feel before going to confession?

2. How do you feel after going to confession?

3. Will you forgive me for _____? (Parents, fill in some offense that you have done, large or small, to your child. If you can't think of anything, your teen would probably be happy to fill in the blank.)

FAMILY APPLICATIONS

1. Once a month, go to confession as a family. By going often, it will remind the members of your family to be forgiving toward each other. Even if it has been 20 years since your last confession, your example will be a powerful witness of humility to your teenager.

2. If you want your children to learn to ask for forgiveness when they fail you, ask forgiveness of your children when you fail them. If you think your teenager has an attention deficit disorder when it comes to listening to you, you will be astonished how attentive he becomes when you ask for his forgiveness.

3. Many people were raised in families where they received more criticism than praise. They believed that the way to achieve acceptance as a son or daughter was to perform flawlessly in sports or academics. Unfortunately, these same people often believe that they must be perfect in order for God to love them. By offering your teen unconditional love, you will help him or her to see that God loves them, independent of their virtues or vices. They learn that they don't need to earn His love, or yours.

4. Many teens who have made sexual mistakes want their parents to know. However, they often hide the truth out of fear or shame. To help create a safe environment for them to open up to you, take an interest in every part of their lives. Reassure them that they can tell you anything. If you talk to your teens about everything (soccer, tests, friends, etc.) it will be a lot easier to talk to them about anything.

5. If you discover that your teen has been sexually active, your emotions might range from deep sorrow or disappointment to complete rage. However, at no other time in his or her life does your teen need to experience your unconditional love more than now. When Christ encountered the woman caught in adultery, it was his profound mercy that allowed her to accept his challenge to go and sin no more (John 8). If a teen feels rejected or condemned, he or she might be tempted to fall further into an unhealthy lifestyle in order to find consolation and acceptance.

Truth and Freedom

I f you were to ask a teenager to describe their idea of perfect freedom, you might hear something like this:

"I want to be able to leave whenever I want, go out with whoever I choose, wear whatever I desire, do whatever I wish, come home when I please ... and then not be asked any questions when I get back." Followed by this litany of demands would be an explanation of why fairness requires you to grant them such freedom. "After all," your teenager may argue, "all my friends get to live like that."

Since teenagers have unique restrictions and responsibilities, they often identify freedom as the absence of rules. In chapter five of *Theology of the Body for Teens*, we aim to expand their narrow concept of human freedom. To do this, we return to the fundamental human desire: love.

In the curriculum, my wife recollects her concept of freedom in high school:

> "Get out of my life!" I screamed and slammed my bedroom door shut. I was so sick of my mother telling me how to live that I couldn't wait until I turned eighteen so I could finally move out. I was tired of her guilt trips and constant nagging about what she thought about my relationship with Andre

I had been in relationships before, but this one was different. We really cared about each other, and since he also came from a broken family, we could relate on many levels. He was a little older than I was, and I was relieved to date a guy who was more mature than most of the boys I knew at our school.

When it came to the sexual stuff, I respected the fact that he'd never push things too far and that he said he was willing to wait until I felt ready. Six months into the relationship, we started sleeping together and I hid it from my mom as long as possible. Eventually, she found some of my birth control pills and went through the roof. I was equally angry with her for invading my privacy and trying to take away my freedom by throwing her religious rules in my face.

But as much as I thought I was fooling my mom, I was only fooling myself. At the time, I thought lying to her and sneaking off with Andre was an expression of my freedom. But if I was so free, then why was I so afraid to leave him, even when the abuse started? If I was so free, why did my hand always tremble when I flipped over a pregnancy test? How could it be that I was doing exactly what I wanted, but I felt so unfulfilled?

Like Crystalina, many teens today long for freedom and love, but end up with neither. One reason why this happens is because teens often abandon the concept of objective truth. In its place, they are drawn toward the idea of moral relativism, where morality becomes a matter of personal opinion. The young person begins to see the Ten Commandments as multiple choice and creates his or her own private system of values.

However, God created us to choose between good and evil, not to determine what they are. Just as we cannot change the law of gravity, we cannot change the moral code that is written in our hearts by God. Such laws have not been created to restrict our freedom, but to help us avoid the slavery of sin.

Love Requires True Freedom

A teen's concept of freedom is the absence of constraints. While this idea of freedom is incomplete, there is some truth to this. For example, in order for a person to be free to love, he or she must be free of internal constraints. An example of an internal constraint involves the tendency that we have to use another person for our selfish desires. Only if a person is freed from this tendency is he or she really able to love another. Just as the desire to love can be disordered and manifested as lust, the desire for freedom can be disordered and manifested in slavery. If you are not free to control your own sexual desires, how can you be free to love?

Being free to love is only possible through the grace of God who gives us pure hearts. Once we choose God and allow Him to transform our desires, then the moral life becomes a life not about rules, but about love. We obey God's commands not because we have to, but because we want to. When teenagers reject the calling to purity and truth (and seek love while pretending to be "free" to do whatever they want), they often end up empty. They have been created by God to become a gift to others and, by doing so, to love as God loves. If they live for themselves, they miss the point of their very existence. And living in this way leaves them unfulfilled.

Although some teens may see the Church's laws regarding premarital sex as an unfair restriction, research shows that girls who are sexually

> "Once the truth is denied to human beings, it is pure illusion to try to set them free. Truth and freedom either go together hand in hand or together they perish in misery."
>
> *- Blessed John Paul II*

active are more than three times as likely to be depressed as girls who are abstinent.[12] Rates of depression among teenage boys who are sexually active are more than twice as high those who are abstinent.[13] In fact, the condition has become so predictable that the *American Journal of Preventive Medicine* recommends to doctors: "[Girls who are engaging in] sexual intercourse should be screened for depression, and provided with anticipatory guidance about the mental health risks of these behaviors."[14] Even if a girl experiments with sex once, research shows an increased risk of depression.[15] These findings show that God's laws are not arbitrary rules created to rob people of freedom. Instead, they have been given to us to help us lead joy-filled lives, trusting in God.

In the words of Blessed John Paul II, "Man longs for love more than for freedom—freedom is the means and love is the end."[16] At some point, a person must surrender certain freedoms in order to make a gift of one's self. However, by doing so, one finds true freedom.

For example, if a husband loves his wife, he should freely choose not to flirt with other women. Instead, he should choose the good of his wife and their marriage over the temptation to commit adultery. If he loves his children, he should freely choose not to neglect them by acting like a bachelor and staying out with friends on a regular basis. With love comes

> "If freedom is not used, is not taken advantage of by love, it becomes a negative thing, and gives human beings a feeling of emptiness and unfulfillment."
>
> *- Blessed John Paul II*

responsibility, which puts the commitments of love into action. But this does not ruin love any more than tying a string on a kite ruins its ability to fly. If you were to cut the string, the kite would crash. The same happens with love. In the words of Blessed John Paul II, "Freedom without responsibilities is the opposite of love."[17] True freedom is not about escaping rules or responsibilities, or reality. True freedom is the ability to desire and to choose the good.

 Questions for Your Teen

1. Sometimes you might feel as if I restrict your freedom. Why do you think I do this?

2. What do you think authentic freedom means?

3. Why might a person who gets to do whatever he wants, whenever he wants, end up being unfulfilled?

4. Do you really believe that God wants you to be free?

1. When you create rules for your teenager, do your best to explain the purpose behind the restrictions. For example, "The reason why I don't want you wearing that belly-button shirt is because I love you, and I know that such an outfit will invite guys to treat you with less respect than you deserve."

2. Always be honest in your dealings with your children, and demand the same honesty in return. Such an environment will create trust and responsibility.

3. Do not doubt yourself as a parent when your teen objects to your rules and restrictions. The only reason you should doubt your parenting abilities would be if your teen actually liked your rules. The day will come when your son or daughter will thank you for your boundaries, but today is probably not that day. Tomorrow is not looking good, either. So, keep up the great work. Your rules have been created by a loving heart, and that is reason enough for you to stand by them.

4. When trying to explain something to your teen, try this technique: Instead of trying to find the most convincing argument, try to ask them the right questions. For example, a teenage girl once told me she was tempted to lose her virginity to a guy she recently met. Instead of giving her a litany of reasons why this would be a terrible decision, I simply asked her, "Why?" She replied, "I don't know." I pressed further, "I want you to really think about this. Why do you want to sleep with him?" "So he'll want me," she answered. "But do you think he wants *you*?" I questioned. "No. He just wants sex," she replied. Because she came up with these answers on her own, she persuaded herself that she didn't want such a guy.

Language of the Body

Teenagers rarely think about sex. Yes, you read that correctly. They talk about it. They joke about it. They listen to songs about it. But how often do teenagers really *think* about sex: What is sex? Who invented it? What is the purpose of sex?

In order to answer these questions, Blessed John Paul II invites us to consider the "language of the body." Without having to say a word, the body is capable of speaking its own language. This can be expressed by something positive like a hug, or negative like a not-so-friendly gesture on the freeway. Since the body is capable of speaking, it is also capable of lying. For example, consider when Judas kissed Jesus while betraying Him (see Mark 14:45). Judas' body said one thing, but his heart clearly said another.

In our sixth chapter, we discuss the body's capacity to speak the truth (or lies) through one's sexuality. If we pause to consider the meaning of sex, its language becomes obvious. One's body is saying, "I am completely yours. I belong totally to you." It is the language spoken by a husband and wife.

However, this language of total self-donation is contradicted by such things as:

- Fornication
- Adultery
- Pornography

- Masturbation
- Contraception

The Empty Promises of Misused Sex

In the case of *fornication* and *adultery*, the bodies of the two people who are not married to one another speak of a total gift of self that does not exist in reality. For example, after the lead character in the movie Vanilla Sky slept with a woman, she said to him, "Don't you know when you sleep with someone ... your body makes a promise whether you do or not?" Odds are, he was not intending to lie to her. But she was right. He had "spoken" a promise with his body that he had not intended.

In the case of *pornography*, there is no union, no relationship, and no true giving of self. The women in the images are not giving themselves in a manner that is for the good of themselves or the other, but are allowing themselves to be used. Those who view them are valuing them for nothing more than their bodies.

Some may argue that "Nobody's getting hurt," but nothing could be further from the truth. Although the images only take a few seconds to see, they take years to forget. Soon, the man's expectations of sexual encounters become distorted. For example, no matter how perfect the model is, the man usually flips the page after a few seconds of viewing. If the image truly satisfied him, he would stop at that page and never turn to another. This is never the case. He always wants more.

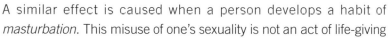

While his standard of physical beauty becomes that of impossible perfection, he experiences arousal followed by boredom and dissatisfaction. But if the most seductive supermodels fail to keep his interest for more than a few moments, what will happen to his bride? How is she expected to captivate him?

Some men think that it's their right to be aroused by fantasies. By the time they get married, they think that marriage is going to be the fulfillment of porn. They may assume, "If my wife isn't flawless, that's kind of her fault." Needless to say, the marriage suffers because the man's ability to love is crippled.

A similar effect is caused when a person develops a habit of *masturbation.* This misuse of one's sexuality is not an act of life-giving love. Instead of training a person in faithfulness and selflessness, masturbation trains a person in selfishness.

> *"Finally, brethren, whatever is true, whatever is honorable, whatever is just, whatever is pure, whatever is lovely, whatever is gracious, if there is any excellence, if there is anything worthy of praise, think about these things."*
>
> *- St. Paul (Phil. 4:8)*

Some examples of the language of the body are clearly "true" or clearly "a lie." Others take more thought and consideration. This is especially true when two people truly appear to love each other in a marriage. So what about the issue of *contraception*? What is a couple saying when they introduce contraception into the marital act?

Surely, spouses who love each other are at least attempting to say in the sexual union, "I am all yours." As we discussed earlier, the giving of oneself in the sexual act is a profound thing. You are saying with your body, "I am totally committed to you—so much so, that I am willing to give you my very person in this most intimate of ways." But in reality, when a couple introduces contraception into their sexual union, they are saying with their bodies, "I refuse to give you all of myself. I won't give you my fertility. I refuse to receive all of you. I won't receive your fertility." Instead of becoming one flesh, they bring a barrier into the act of sex—a barrier between their full love and gift of self.

> *"The Church and the world today more than ever need married couples and families who generously let themselves be schooled by Christ."*
>
> *- Blessed John Paul II*

Whether a person is married or not, it is challenging to practice the virtue of chastity. Using the gift of our sexuality according to God's designs is demanding. However, the whole power of temptation rests on the deceptive promise that living for ourselves will give us more joy than if we live for God.

> *"Love, to be real, must cost—it must hurt—it must empty us of self."*
>
> *- Blessed Mother Teresa of Calcutta*

Questions for Your Teen

1. If you hope to get married one day, would you want your future spouse to look at pornographic images?

2. If you hope to get married one day, would you want your future spouse to experience sexual intimacy with people other than you?

3. Does it make sense to you that the sexual act is more than just a physical activity, but rather "speaks a language"?

4. What are some other examples of how the body can tell truths or tell lies?

FAMILY APPLICATIONS

1. Have you, as a married couple, learned the reasons behind the Church's stance on family planning? If not, Christopher West's book *Good News About Sex and Marriage* is a great place to start.

2. When a parent practices the virtues of purity, obedience, and humility, the children are far more likely to follow after their example. This is because virtues are more easily caught than they are taught.

3. To help prevent your teen from being influenced by a culture saturated with lust, put an internet filter on your computer (See appendix). Also, learn to check your history files on your computer, to make sure that no one has been visiting pornographic web sites. Another good idea is to keep the computer in a high-traffic area of the house and facing the traffic flow. If your teen has a Facebook, Twitter, or MySpace page, visit it often, and make sure the profile is set to private, so that strangers cannot contact your teen.

4. A teenager once said, "I entirely failed at chastity because I could never answer the question, 'Why wait?'" Have you given your teens solid answers to such a question? If not, consider the resources available at Chastity.com.

5. According to the *American Journal of Public Health*, teens are more likely to become sexually active if they think their parents approve of birth control.[18] Expect your teen to practice abstinence until marriage, and do not give in to the world's idea that teens are "going to do it anyway." Instead, show them that you have confidence in their ability to practice self control and make smart decisions. According to the Centers for Disease Control, most high school students are virgins, and the trend toward abstinence is growing.[19]

Chapter
Seven

Free, Total, Faithful, Fruitful

Young people often dream of finding the perfect love. However, they do not spend a great deal of time learning how to give true love.

In the first half of our curriculum, we discussed how your teenager should understand his or her identity as a person made to give and receive love, in the image and likeness of God. Now, we delve into more specifics about how to express that love.

From the beginning of the Bible to the end, there is one analogy that God uses above all others to express His love for us: the love between a husband and wife. The story of God's love in the Bible begins in Genesis with the marriage of Adam and Eve and concludes with the book of Revelation in which we read about the marriage of the Lamb—the union of Christ and the Church in heaven. The reality is that when the love of a bride and groom is a total gift, it makes God's love visible to the world. God's love for us is *free, total, faithful*, and *life-giving*, and so should be the couple's love for each other. In fact, these four aspects of love (free, total, faithful, and fruitful) are mirrored in the vows and promises that a husband and wife exchange during their wedding.

However, consider what happens when you take these vows as they apply to one's sexuality—and then flip them upside down:

- Instead of sex being *free*, it is pressured at the end of a date, forced in sexual abuse, paid for in prostitution, and not freely given by the person dominated by lust.

- Instead of a *total* gift of self, there are one-night stands where there is no real commitment to the other and supposedly "safe" sex, where the couple is more concerned with protecting themselves than giving themselves.

- Instead of promoting chastity and *fidelity*, Hollywood celebrates casual sex.

- Instead of being *fruitful*, the act of sex is sterilized with contraception and is not open to the possibility of new life.

If you remove one leg from a chair, it will collapse. In the same way, if you remove any one of these four essential elements of married love from the gift of sex, it will no longer be a true gift. As a result, those having sexual encounters outside of marriage find themselves unfulfilled. No amount of pleasure alone can satisfy a person, because we have been created to give ourselves totally and receive the other totally. Anything less will never satisfy.

This vision of human sexuality is not a list of four rules the Church forces us to follow. These are the demands of love already written on our hearts and stamped into our bodies. And if

> "[A young heart feels] a desire for greater generosity, more commitment, greater love. This desire for more is a characteristic of youth; a heart that is in love does not calculate, does not begrudge, it wants to give of itself without measure."
>
> *- Blessed John Paul II*

we live out this call to love through a sincere gift of self, we become a visible image of Christ's love for the Church.

The Church & Sex

Many people assume that the Church is down on sex. This could not be further from the truth. Here's just one small example of the thousands that exist. Did you know that the canopy (baldacchino) often built over the altar in Catholic churches is similar to the canopy over a marriage bed? The symbolism reminds us that on the altar during Mass, the Bridegroom (Christ) gives His body (the Eucharist) to His bride (the Church), so that we may have eternal life. Likewise, as a husband and wife renew their love and wedding vows through their life-giving one-flesh union on their marriage bed, we renew our love and our union with Christ when we pronounce "Amen" and receive His body. St. Paul spoke of this deep symbolism when he wrote, "'For this reason a man shall leave his father and mother and be joined to his wife, and the two shall become one.' This is a great mystery, and I mean in reference to Christ and the church" (Eph 5:31-32).

In a similar way, a husband and wife express their love for each other through their *free, total, faithful*, and *fruitful* gift of themselves.

Therefore, this call to love is not only stamped into our bodies but also into the body *of Christ* in the Eucharist! This is not sexualizing the Eucharist. This is realizing the sacredness of sex. So the real question to ask when it comes to sexual morality is this: Am I expressing God's love in and through my body?

However, we cannot give what we do not possess. St. Bernard once observed that only when a reservoir fills up with water can it then overflow into the valleys and fields surrounding it, bringing life to all.[20] This image reflects our call to love. Only when we fill up with God's love, receiving all that He wants to give us, will we have the gift to offer another (a spouse or the Church) the gift of God's love.

> *"Real love is demanding. I would fail in my mission if I did not tell you so. Love demands a personal commitment to the will of God."*
>
> *- Blessed John Paul II*

The future of our young people rests upon their openness toward and understanding of God's will for their lives. As they head toward the vocation of marriage or toward studies in a seminary or convent, they should consider the fact that unless they learn to receive the love of God, they will be unable to give love to others. But once they have received His love, they will be prepared to live it freely, totally, faithfully, and fruitfully.

> *"There is no place for selfishness—and no place for fear! Do not be afraid, then, when love makes demands. Do not be afraid when love requires sacrifice."*
>
> *- Blessed John Paul II*

Questions for Your Teen

1. If so many teens want true love, why do you think so many of them settle for unloving relationships?

2. Why do you think it is so hard for some people to be faithful?

3. What is unsafe about "safe" sex? (Hint: Look beyond STD and pregnancy risks to the emotional, spiritual, and relational consequences of sexual activity).

1. Just as an intern learns by watching a professional at work, children learn to love by watching their parents. If the words, "I love you," "I'm sorry," and "I forgive you," are spoken often at home, the children will be given a durable foundation on which to build their own families one day.

2. Consider how many ways you can express your wedding vows to your spouse without having to say a word. One such example would be to exercise the vow of faithfulness. Today, many people assume that they fulfill the promise of fidelity by avoiding affairs. However, one must also be faithful in his or her imagination. "Fidelity of the eyes and heart" is essential for true love to flourish.

Chapter Eight

Marriage

It has been estimated that the average couple spends 200 hours preparing for their wedding day. Considering that half of all marriages end in divorce, it makes one wonder how much time the average couple spends preparing for their married life. Although many couples are required to attend marriage preparation classes before the big day, much more is needed than a few hours of preparation. If a high school student hopes to enter the sacrament of marriage one day, it's important that he or she not wait until the months or weeks before the wedding to gain a rich understanding and develop the skills necessary for building a healthy relationship.

Therefore, in chapter eight of *Theology of the Body for Teens: High School Edition* we focus on the meaning of marriage, and the skills necessary to create lasting love. Sadly, many teenagers today see so many broken marriages that they no longer view marriage as a goal or dream. We invite especially these students to look beyond such failed marriages and have the courage to see God's original plan for the great sacrament.

In the first chapter, we discussed how God is a communion of persons (Father, Son, and Holy Spirit) united in love, and that we are made in

> *"If two pieces of wood are carefully glued together, their union will be so close that it is easier to break them in some fresh place than where they were joined; and God so unites man and wife, that it is easier to sever soul and body than those two."*
>
> *- St. Francis de Sales*

His image and likeness. When we live out our vocation to love, we become a reflection of God Himself.

This sounds like a nice, holy concept, but what does it really mean for the teen who anticipates marriage? Blessed John Paul II taught us that marriage (and family life) is a "school of love." In the words of St. Francis De Sales, marriage is a "perpetual exercise of mortification," adding that "occasions for suffering are more frequent in this state than in any other." Some people would complain that this makes marriage look like death. In a way, they're right—but deaths also come with resurrections. In fact, anything worthwhile requires sacrifice (playing organized sports, getting a good job, doing well in school). Marriage is the best place on earth to learn how to sacrifice for the sake of the other. At the core of this training is learning to die to one's self. It is precisely in this offering—in the death of one's own desires—that true love comes to life.

The Essence of Love is Sacrifice

For this reason, Christians have always looked to the relationship between Christ and his Church as the model of love for married couples. In fact, Blessed John Paul II insisted that this spousal analogy is the only way to understand the sacrament of marriage.

In his letter to the Ephesians, St. Paul writes, "Husbands, love your wives, as Christ loved the church and gave himself up for her" (Eph 5:25). He declares that a husband should be willing to serve his wife unto the point of death. Such a noble spirit is often alive in the hearts of couples who have just fallen in love. However, it often fades as the years draw on. I once heard a wife say, "When we first got married, my husband said he would lay down his life for me. Now that we have been married 20 years, he won't even lay down the remote control to talk to me."

It isn't easy to maintain a heroic spirit of love, but it is possible. In every relationship, a time of testing arises. Sometimes, it is early in the marriage, when the infatuation begins to fade. Love is placed in a crucible of stress or suffering, and its value is revealed. Blessed John Paul II tells us that at this point, "If their love is a true gift of self, so that they belong to the other, it will not only survive but grow stronger, and sink deeper roots."[21] But if the two people do not see the value of sacrificial love and rely on superficial benefits and emotions, they often quickly run from the challenges.

Perhaps most importantly, teenagers must learn that successful marriages are not based upon *finding* the perfect person, but upon *loving* the imperfect person they have chosen to marry. It is essential that young people learn these principles, so that they are not shocked when the honeymoon ends. If they have the courage and faith to persevere through the

difficult times, a more beautiful form of love will appear.

With the high rate of divorce, it is easy for teens today to think that marriage is nothing more than a contract on a piece of paper, but this is not the case. Marriage was and is God's idea. He created it, and He reveals Himself to our world through the love of a husband and wife.

> *"There is no relationship between human beings so close as that of husband and wife, if they are united as they ought to be."*
>
> *- St. John Chrysostom*

To help renew the students' faith in the hope of lasting love, we remind them of the Old Testament story of Tobias and Sarah. As they were praying together on their wedding night, Sarah's father was digging a grave for her new husband! She had been married seven times before, and every single groom died on the wedding night. So Sarah's dad figured that he would save some time and start digging a hole for Tobias.

> *"In the Bible, the man-woman couple is not meant to be simply a preservation of the species, as is the case for the other animals. Insofar as it was called to become the image and likeness of God, it expresses in a bodily, tangible way the face of God, which is Love."*
>
> *- Cardinal Carlo Martini*

Thankfully, God protected Tobias and gave him a long life with his bride. But just as Sarah's previous marriages all ended in death, perhaps many of the marriages in and around your family have been broken in one way or another. We remind the students that this need not be the case with their own marriage, should they hope to enter one.

Questions for Your Teen

1. Do you hope to get married one day?

2. When do you think is a smart time to get married? (At this point, feel free to remind them that, biologically speaking, the part of the human brain that makes important decisions is not fully mature until the mid 20s.)

3. What do you think you can do now to help make sure your marriage will last?

4. Do you think you'll have a lasting marriage?

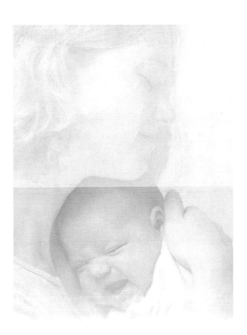

1. The greatest lesson about marriage will not come from our curriculum, but from the eighteen years your son or daughter will spend living with you. Every act of self-denial, patience, mercy, and tenderness expressed between you and your spouse will speak more eloquently than anything your child will ever read.

2. If your marriage has ended for whatever reason, make sure that your son or daughter has the opportunity to spend time with married relatives or friends who have strong relationships.

3. If your family prays grace at meals, or offers a family rosary, perhaps you could include a prayer intention for the future spouses of your children, in case they hope to get married one day. This will help your teens envision the future, and help them see that they are not simply waiting for a sacrament, but for a specific person. Such a concept will also help them realize there is more to life than passing high school relationships. Encourage your teens to prepare themselves now to become someone their future spouse would deserve.

4. Many parents *pray* for their teens, but few *fast* for them. Do not overlook the power of fasting (Mark 9:29).

Chapter Nine

Celibacy and Religious Life

If you were to ask most teenage boys what keeps them from considering the priesthood, the answer would be quite simple: "I like girls." They operate, in part, under the presumption that those who enter the religious life must be androgynous beings who are not attracted to anyone but God. As a result, having a vocation to the priesthood seems inconceivable. Many girls make a similar presumption: "Oh, I could never be a nun. I want to have kids." They assume that women who become nuns must not want to become mothers.

Although these ideas are obviously misconceptions, there is a fundamental truth in them: God stamped into every human heart the desire for spousal union and life-giving love. The presence of these longings is often fulfilled through the sacrament of marriage. However, it is also fulfilled through a life of celibacy, offered to God.

All men are called to be a husband and father in some way, and every woman is called in some way to be a wife and mother. These desires do not exclude people or give them a reason to disqualify themselves from a religious calling. These desires

> *"Priesthood is the love of the heart of Jesus. When you see a priest, think of our Lord Jesus Christ."*
>
> St. John Vianney

are placed within us for a reason. There is a reason that priests are called "Father." There is a reason why the famous little nun from Calcutta was called "Mother." Both of them begot (generated) many spiritual children by their union with Christ and the Church. So, the real question is: How is God calling each of us to live out these desires to be husband/father or wife/mother?

Everyone is Called to "Marriage"

As the teachers of this curriculum discuss the religious life with your teen, the first thing we mention to them is that everyone on earth is called to marriage. This may seem like a strange way to begin a chapter on celibacy, but it's true. When a priest is ordained, he chooses to marry the Church as his bride. When a woman enters the consecrated life, she is being espoused by Christ Himself. Like a bride, she wears a veil as a visible sign of her marital union with Jesus. Among other things, these expressions of the celibate vocation are reminders that heaven will be an eternal wedding celebration between God and His bride, the Church.

"Some are incapable of marriage because they were born so; some, because they were made so by others; some, because they have renounced marriage for the sake of the kingdom of heaven. Whoever can accept this ought to accept it"

- Matthew 19:12

Here on earth, married couples are a sacramental sign that points to this eternal reality. When we get to heaven, earthly marriages will give way to the heavenly reality. So, when a person chooses to be celibate for the sake of the kingdom instead of the sacrament of matrimony, he or she is basically skipping the sacrament (the sign), and, in a very real way, living the

> *"A lack of vocations follows from the breakdown of the family, yet where parents are generous in welcoming life, children will be more likely to be generous when it comes to the question of offering themselves to God."*
>
> *- Pontifical Council for the Family, The Truth and Meaning of Human Sexuality*

eternal reality to which the sacrament pointed: undivided union with God.

To live a celibate life offered to God is an exceptional calling. Unfortunately, many people do not appreciate the value of such a life. All too often, people think of celibacy as something a person is *not* doing with their sexuality. This view misses the point of celibacy. Those who enter the religious life as priests, brothers, religious sisters, and such are a foreshadowing of how all of us will live in the heavenly kingdom. In heaven, being in the presence of God will far exceed any earthly joy. Celibacy is a witness to the fact that there is a greater joy—heaven—than the joys of this world. Celibates do not reject their sexuality. They're showing us the ultimate purpose and meaning of sexuality: the giving of ourselves to God. In their decision to renounce marriage on earth, celibates embrace their sexuality and channel that energy toward full communion with God, reflecting in a unique way the meaning of sexuality and self-donation.

Through their total dedication to Christ, men and women in the religious life point us to the ultimate purpose of our lives: union with God. They also show us how to get there by making a sincere gift of ourselves in love. In Chapter Three of this curriculum, we discussed with your student the spousal meaning of the body. We learned that our bodies reveal our calling to make a total gift of ourselves in love. It's obvious how a married couple makes a gift of themselves, but what about a celibate man or woman? When a person enters the religious life,

> "Young people know that their life has meaning to the extent that it becomes a gift for others."
>
> -Blessed John Paul II

he or she does exactly this. They totally dedicate their lives to the service of God and humanity and offer themselves at our service. They teach us God's word and His love through the corporal works of mercy, through the sacraments, and through spiritual works of mercy.

> "Religious orders are not formed for the purpose of gathering perfect people, but for those who have the courage to aim at perfection."
>
> - St. Francis de Sales

Some people are turned off by the idea of the religious life because they think, "I just can't imagine not having sex." If teens think of marriage as an outlet for lust or sexual tension, they're bound to think of the religious life as sexual repression. They should realize, though, that both the married person and the celibate person must have dominion over his or her lust. When people are in control of their sexuality, only then are they capable of making a gift of themselves. This gift can be given to a spouse, or it can be offered as a sacrifice for the Kingdom through celibacy.

Questions for your Teen:

1. Have you ever thought about a vocation to the religious life?

2. Do you think it is possible to be truly happy without getting married?

3. Why do you think people have lost the sense of how great the celibate vocation really is?

4. What do you think would be some of the benefits of becoming a priest or nun?

5. What can be done—by the Church—to effectively communicate the value of the celibate vocation?

1. Some parents think, "I don't want my kid to be a priest or nun. I want grandchildren." Are you open to the possibility that God might be calling one of your children to serve him through the celibate life?

2. Visit a local convent of nuns, and bring your teen with you. Or, invite religious over for dinner on a regular basis so your kids can get used to being around professed religious and learning about their lives and their calling. Get to know some of the sisters, and ask for their prayers. In return, offer to pray for their specific intentions as well.

3. The media often mocks priesthood and the religious life. Make sure that your children know that this is unacceptable. Furthermore, be sure never to criticize your own priest. Should there be a need to address a particular issue, your teens should know that it should always be done with reverence and great respect.

Finding Your Vocation

Vocation discernment. These are not two words most teens are "Googling" and Instant Messaging about late at night. However, more than any other time in life, the teenage years are spent wondering about one's identity and future. For this reason, teens need to know how to hear God's calling in their lives.

The word vocation comes from the Latin *vocare*, meaning "to call." If we all have a call (which we all do), then we all must figure out what that call from God is. As a parent, your calling has already been made clear. Your teenager, however, has just begun to chart his or her future.

In the last two chapters, we discussed the different vocations to which God may call your teen in order to make a gift of himself or herself. But how do they know which path God is calling them to follow? God seems to call most people to the sacrament of marriage. But how can a teenager know his or her

> *"One drawback of a society dominated by technology and the mass media is the fact that silence becomes increasingly difficult to achieve."*
>
> *- Blessed John Paul II*

> *"When it is God who is speaking ... the proper way to behave is to imitate someone who has an irresistible curiosity and who listens at keyholes. You must listen to everything God says at the keyhole of your heart."*
>
> *- St. John Vianney*

calling for sure? Furthermore, how is one to know who to marry?

The answers to such will determine the rest of one's life. So, how is a teenager to decide? We suggest the first step is to learn how to listen to God. However, teens often make this normally simple action pretty difficult. Here are five reasons it can be hard for a teenager to hear His voice:

Too Noisy: Teens wake up to music, watch television over breakfast, listen to the radio in the car, talk all day, and then go home to the internet, video games, the phone, and more television. Some teens even do some of these things while sleeping! None of these activities are bad in themselves, but if they could just turn off some of the noise, they would find it easier to be still and quiet in prayer. The same goes for us adults. In the words of Blessed John Paul II, "Above all, create silence in your interior. Let that ardent desire to see God arise from the depth of your hearts, a desire that at times is suffocated by the noise of the world and the seduction of pleasures."[22]

Really Busy: Many teens (and adults) wait until they have the time to pray, and that time never comes. We often complain that we have no time to pray, but the average American spends between seven and ten years of his or her life watching TV! Like any good relationship, our friendship with God will deepen according to how much effort we put into it. Therefore, we

encourage the teens (and you) to set a daily prayer time, and stick to it. Morning and night prayers are a good place to start. Set your alarm clock ten minutes early each day, and reserve that time to say some morning prayers, read the Bible and talk with God. One of Blessed John Paul II's most vivid childhood memories was when he walked by his father's room and saw his father kneeling, lost in prayer. If we want our teens to pray well, we must lead the way by our silent example.

Scared Stiff: Many teens don't trust God, and they're afraid to hear what He has to say. Maybe He's asking them to let go of something or do something that's really hard—and they don't want to listen.

Don't Care: Many teens are simply indifferent. For any number of reasons, they don't care what God has to say. Some are being raised in homes where faith plays little role. Others have been entertained to death with the toys of the world. Some have experienced great suffering that has caused them to doubt God's love. Still others have lived lives of such comfort that they have not felt the need to rely on God.

> *"Every vocation, every path to which Christ calls us, ultimately leads to fulfillment and happiness, because it leads to God, to sharing in God's own life."*
>
> *- Blessed John Paul II*

Blurry Vision: Our sins make it hard for us to see clearly. When we sin, it is almost as if we place a dirty window between ourselves and God. Each time we turn from Him, we add to the dirt. Before long, we can barely see through it. And very little light comes in to us from the other side. Then, we complain that we don't see God in our lives. Especially when we commit sexual sins, the mind seems to fill up with such worldly thoughts that we are unable to recognize the voice of God. But the Sacrament of Reconciliation serves as a potent cleanser to wash away the dirt and make the panes of the window clear for us to see God.

These tips on listening to God's voice apply to each of us, regardless of our age or marital status. If we begin to create silence in our lives, make time to pray, trust God, and avoid sin, it will be much easier to listen to what God has to say. Through prayer, we come to know and trust Him. And only if we trust Him will we pay attention enough to know His plan for our lives.

No matter what one's vocation is, we are all called to a life of holiness. No one's life is an accident. God has created each of us for a reason. The ultimate reason for His creating us is to share his own eternal bliss with us in heaven.

Questions for Your Teen

1. Why do you think many of the great saints say that silence is so important?

2. How much time do you spend in silence?

3. Do you believe God has a specific plan for your life? If so, what do you think it could be?

4. Do you trust God?

1. Invite your parish priest to bless your house and share dinner with you. This will give your family an opportunity to know him on a more personal level. You could ask him about his day-to-day life, and how he felt the call to become a priest. Such a conversation would be invaluable in helping a young man to consider his vocation.

2. If your son or daughter has shown an interest in the religious life, help him or her to attend a local discernment retreat.

3. We noted five reasons why it is difficult for teens to hear the voice of God. Consider how you could overcome some of these obstacles. For example, to create more silence, encourage your teenager to give up music for Lent. To give your teen extra incentive to give it a shot, say, "In return, I'll let you decide what I should give up for Lent that will be just as much of a challenge for me." If they say, "oxygen," don't take it personally.

Dating with Purpose and Purity

With a sack lunch in his hand and a science book tucked under his arm, a seventh grade boy approached me after I spoke at his middle school. In a cracking voice that signaled the dawn of puberty, he inquired, "I started dating this one girl when we were in third grade, and we were pretty serious for three years. I broke up with her last year, and now I'm wondering if I should ask out this other girl." After I gave him what advice I could (which, of course, included the fact that a seventh grader should be focused on school and other pursuits), I pondered what a "pretty serious" relationship meant to a pair of eight-year-olds.

There's no denying it: teens today live in a world where everyone seems to have a date … except for them. Girls are the ones who suffer the most from this modern phenomenon because the guys are the ones who traditionally make the first move. So, if no guy is leaving text messages on a girl's phone, she will assume that she is not only incomplete but defective. After all, if she doesn't have a date, there must be a reason, right? It may not even occur to her that most guys

> *"'Purity?' they ask. And they smile. They are the ones who go on to marriage with worn-out bodies and disillusioned souls."*
>
> - St. Josemaria Escriva

are either too wrapped up in their video games or too shy to ask.

But there is no use comforting her. In her mind, she is alone. She is unlikable. Nobody pursues her because she's unlovable. She will probably grow old alone and live with twelve cats.

To help girls—as well as guys— overcome this phobia of not having a boyfriend or girlfriend for a week, we explore the purpose of dating in chapter eleven of the curriculum.

A New "Dating" Paradigm

The modern practice of dating is really less than a hundred years old. Before the car was around, a man would usually "court" a woman in the presence of her family, with the hope of marrying her. Once the car was invented, the family was pretty much cut out of the dating scene because a guy usually could just pick up a girl at her house and leave. With the family largely out of the picture, dating with the goal of marriage soon fell out of sight. And before long, dating became something to do for recreation.

With this "recreational" approach to relationships, a person ends up breaking up with each person he or she dates ... except for the one who becomes that person's spouse. We invite the teens to consider, "Does this sound like good preparation for a lifelong marriage?" A common

> *"We must never forget that only when love between human beings is put to the test can its true value be seen."*
>
> *- Blessed John Paul II*

> *"Love ...*
> *is victorious*
> *because it prays."*
>
> *- Blessed John Paul II*

response might be, "Yes, because you get to see what type of person you like and can, therefore, make a better choice someday." Perhaps, but the downsides to this approach far outweigh this possible benefit. Here is why: For one, the ultimate purpose of dating is to find a spouse. If a teen dates for recreation, he or she is just training himself/herself in the habit of failed relationships. For this reason, we do not recommend teens date anyone whom they cannot see themselves marrying, and to never date a person expecting that he or she will change.

Some people assume that there's no reason *not* to date in high school. However, a study of over eight hundred high school students was conducted to determine how their dating age impacted their sexual behavior. Here's what was found: Among the teens who began dating in seventh grade, only 29 percent of boys and 10 percent of girls were still virgins at the time they were interviewed. However, of those who waited until they were sixteen years old to date, 84 percent of boys and 82 percent of girls were still virgins.[23]

Casual dating—versus the more purposeful concept of "courting"— creates a much higher probability that the relationship will involve sexual activity. As your teen will see throughout this program, this comes with a whole host of spiritual, emotional, and psychological problems. In short, unmarried sexually active relationships are recipes for disaster.

Teens who delay dating seem to end up better off. They don't have a string of soap opera relationships and emotional divorces. They also gain several added benefits. For example, they develop greater independence, learn to relate to the opposite sex as friends, and are given more of a chance to discover their identity, goals, and dreams.

> *"Only the chaste man and the chaste woman are capable of true love."*
>
> *- Blessed John Paul II*

Planning for Success

Besides explaining the purpose of dating, we also offer your teens advice on how to keep their relationships pure. Here is a list of ten suggestions we will offer them:

1. Pray for purity every morning. Don't repress sexual desires, but pray for their redemption. Three Hail Marys are a great way to do this.

2. Avoid impure relationships before they begin.

3. Once you are in a relationship, avoid places and situations in which you're likely to fall into sin.

4. Know your boundaries before you're tempted, and make sure your date knows them before you even date the person. This may mean you need to have a specific discussion about it.

5. Choose friends who will help you grow in purity.

6. Double date or group date with friends who have high standards.

7. Get rid of impure music, magazines, and TV shows. St. Paul tells us, "If there is any excellence and if there is anything worthy of praise, think about these things" (Phil 4:8, NAB).

8. Listen to the advice of your wisest friends and family members who are committed Christians.

9. Try to go to confession at least once a month.

10. Lastly, if things are going too far, do not be afraid to say "No."

For a teen to understand the point of chastity, he or she needs to understand its relation to love. By practicing purity, a couple is doing what is best for the other, and is sacrificing to bring about a greater union than passing pleasure would offer. If a teen does not understand this, he or she may be willing to risk pregnancy, heartbreak, or STDs in an effort to love and be loved. Explain to your teenager that finding happiness through purity is not about merely saying no to sexual activity, but rather saying yes to love. By living the pure life, teenagers can enjoy good friendships now, while preparing for a future of happiness and romance without regret.

> *"Don't say, 'That's the way I am—it's my character.' It's your lack of character. Esto vir!—Be a man!"*
>
> *- St. Josemaria Escriva*

Questions for Your Teen

1. Do you want to date in high school? Explain why or why not.

2. What do you think is the purpose of dating? And, do you think there is a point of dating in high school?

3. If your future spouse were dating someone else right now, how physically intimate would you want them to be with that person?

4. What percentage of the relationships at your school do you think will lead to marriage?

1. If you are watching a movie or TV show with your family, and the story line distorts love or healthy relationships, consider using this as a teachable moment. Feel free to wax eloquent to your teenagers about why premarital sex in sitcoms is hardly an expression of love. Even though your teens may protest about hearing your commentary, you are sharpening their consciences. That way, if they see distorted ideas and images in the future, they will remember that these are counterfeits. And hopefully, they'll change the channel.

2. When discussing sexual morality, the responsibility should be shared by the mother and the father. If the father is silent, the teens may very well assume that he disagrees with the mother, but is being polite by staying quiet.

3. Discuss with your spouse an appropriate age to allow your children to start dating/courting. For example, my wife and I recently had our first daughter. After a few weeks of deliberation, I have concluded that thirty-six is an appropriate and reasonable age for her to begin dating.

4. Keep tabs on your teen's friends. As Saint Paul said, "Bad company ruins good morals" (1 Cor 15:33). Research backs this up: when half or more of a teen's friends are sexually active, that teen is thirty-one times as likely to get drunk and twenty-two times as likely to have smoked pot compared with teens who don't hang out with sexually active friends.[24] Another study showed, "only 4 percent of young people whose friends were not sexually active were sexually active themselves. Amongst those whose friends *were* sexually active, the figure was 43 percent."[25]

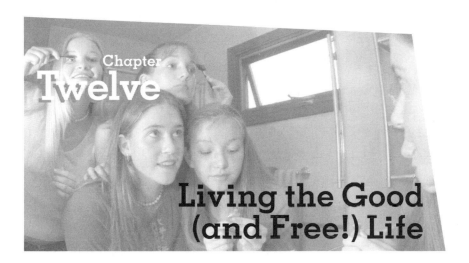

Chapter Twelve

Living the Good (and Free!) Life

A ll too often, doctrines taught in religion class stay in the classroom. A teenager might get an A+ on a religion test but may not see any practical way that the material affects his or her daily life. One of the great realities of the Theology of the Body is its ability to transform people's lives if they grasp and apply what is being taught.

The reason the Theology of the Body is able to do this is because it gives a new lens through which we can see ourselves, the world, and eternity. In this new understanding, teens discover the truth that sets them free. After learning the material, only one thing remains: for the teen to make a personal response, and live out these truths.

In our final chapter of *Theology of the Body for Teens*, we invite teens to look back on the past eleven lessons. What we learn with Blessed John Paul II's analysis of creation is that God created us for love. We find this truth—that we were created for love stamped in our bodies. We discover in our own bodies that "man was not meant to be alone" but, rather, that we were called to give ourselves to another in love. This is what is meant by the phrase *spousal* meaning of our bodies. Our bodies also point us to our destiny: our eternal communion with God.

The teaching on original sin reveals that man suffers from concupiscence. The church's teaching on original sin reveals that man

> *"When you decide firmly to lead a clean life, chastity will not be a burden on you: it will be a crown of triumph."*
>
> *- St. Josemaria Escriva*

suffers from concupiscence (the inclination to sin). As a result, we must struggle to love each other with truth and integrity. Even still, purity is possible. Because of the grace won for us on the Cross through Christ's death and resurrection, we can overcome vice to a substantial degree in this life and richly fulfill our call to love. Christ does not condemn us for our past. Instead, He heals us and gives us strength to overcome temptation and to live a life of grace, to overcome shame, and find the freedom that comes through purity of heart.

In John Paul II's explanation of our heavenly calling, we discover that union with God is the ultimate fulfillment of everything for which we have been created. In heaven we will experience the joy that comes from giving the total gift of ourselves and a radical reception of God's very life. Through this experience, we will be consumed in the perfect heavenly marriage between Christ and the Church. We will be fulfilled beyond all human expectation.

Living the Language of the Body in Truth

Realizing there is a specific language of the body that we speak helps us to pay attention to the "words" we speak through our actions. The task of our lives is to learn to speak the language of the body as God intended: *freely, totally, faithfully,* and *fruitfully.* It is a challenge, to be sure, but also

provides us with the opportunity to be schooled in the art of love. Living this life of virtue will not only lead us to happiness, but to holiness.

When we learn to live faithfully and to love rightly, we will have peace as we discern the path that God is asking us to walk. We will know that our joy comes from giving ourselves completely to God, regardless of the vocation to which we're called. If we love and live entirely for God, we will fulfill the purpose for which we were created! We will be living according to the truth of who we are—a truth that will set us free (see John 8:32).

Being made in God's image and likeness is the starting point. Receiving God's love and loving others through self-giving is the path. And union with God in heaven is the destination. If teens allow these truths to sink in, it will transform the way they view life itself.

Living the Truth

But life is not simply *viewed*. Life is *lived*. While the need to "give of yourself" may not be hard to understand, putting this truth into practice is another matter. Teens can live out this calling through·

- **Corporal works of mercy.** Some corporal works of mercy include: feeding the hungry, giving drink to the thirsty, sheltering the homeless,

> *"Virtue can only come from spiritual strength."*
>
> *- Blessed John Paul II*

clothing the naked, and visiting the sick.

- **Evangelization.** Although the concept of evangelization may be intimidating to some, many teens spread the gospel by sharing their testimony, leading retreats, etc. We encourage the teens to do this by looking to the words of St. Catherine of Siena, who said "If you are what you should be, you will set the whole world ablaze!"

> *"Love Our Lady. And she will obtain for you abundant grace to conquer in your daily struggle."*
>
> *- St. Josemaria Escriva*

- **Living by example.** As St. Francis said, "Preach the Gospel at all times and when necessary use words."

- **Remembering one's goodness.** All too often, teens focus on their imperfections instead of realizing how God sees them.

- **Learning the faith.** We cannot give what we do not possess. Therefore, in order to share the faith, we need to learn it.

- **Beginning and ending the day with prayer:** Blessed (Mother) Teresa of Calcutta said, "Purity is the fruit of prayer." In prayer, one gains the interior strength to turn the tide from impurity to purity, from selfishness to generosity, from lust to love.

> *"Holy purity is granted by God when it is asked for with humility."*
>
> *- St. Josemaria Escriva*

When students leave their religion classes, they will be bombarded by misleading commercials, peers, billboards, and pop-up ads. In order to resist the negative influences, students need a moral compass, a well-formed conscience, a foundation of truth. The Theology of the Body provides this. By allowing its message to penetrate their hearts, young people today will be able to fulfill the Holy Father's challenge to them:

> "Remember: Christ is calling you; the Church needs you; the Blessed believes in you and he expects great things of you!"[26] "Young people of every continent, do not be afraid to be the saints of the new millennium! Be contemplative, love prayer; be coherent with your faith and generous in the service of your brothers and sisters, be active members of the Church and builders of peace. To succeed in this demanding project of life, continue to listen to His Word, draw strength from the Sacraments, especially the Eucharist and Penance. The Lord wants you to be intrepid apostles of his Gospel and builders of a new humanity."[27]

 Questions for Your Teen

1. What was the most important thing you learned from the curriculum?

2. Does it give you hope or weigh you down?

3. Have you ever shared your faith?

4. Have you ever needed to defend your faith? Were you prepared for the challenge?

5. Do you desire to live out this teaching?

1. Perform works of mercy as a family. For example, bring food to the homeless or visit sick relatives or friends.

2. Perform spiritual works of mercy within the family: Some of these include: counseling the doubtful, comforting the sorrowful, bearing wrongs patiently, forgiving all injuries, and praying for the living and the dead.

3. Teach your children the faith. Do not leave this responsibility to the priests or the teachers. You don't need a theology degree to do this. However, if you feel that you are unprepared for the task, make the time to learn the faith. Studying the *Catechism of the Catholic Church* is a great place to start. There are also many great online resources, such as www.catholic.com and www.newadvent.org.

4. Help your sons and daughters spend time with good role models. Young people often look up to celebrities or athletes who rarely exemplify the Christian lifestyle. Therefore, if you know of any relatives, youth ministers, teachers, or neighbors who might set a good example, try to make time for your teen to interact with these individuals. It's essential that young people have concrete examples of normal and happy people living holy lives.

NOTES

[1] National Campaign to Prevent Teen Pregnancy, "With One Voice 2004: America's Adults and Teens Sound Off About Teen Pregnancy."

[2] *Gaudium et Spes*, no. 24.

[3] National Campaign to Prevent Teen Pregnancy, "With One Voice 2004: Americas Adults and Teens Sound Off About Teen Pregnancy."

[4] Message of the Holy Father John Paul II to the Youth of the World on the Occasion of the XIX World Youth Day 2004, February 22, 2004.

[5] Karol Wojtyla (Blessed John Paul II), *Love and Responsibility* (San Francisco: Ignatius, 1993), 131.

[6] Christopher West, *Good About Sex and Marriage* (Ann Arbor, MI: Servant, 2000), 29.

[7] *Love and Responsibility*, 171.

[8] Blessed John Paul II, general audience, November 24, 1982. As quoted by *Man and Woman He Created Them*, 519.

[9] *Love and Responsibility*, 181.

[10] National Campaign to Prevent Teen Pregnancy, "With One Voice 2003: Americas Adults and Teens Sound Off About Teen Pregnancy."

[11] Message of the Holy Father John Paul II to the Youth of the World on the Occasion of the XIX World Youth Day 2004, February 22, 2004.

[12] Robert E. Rector, et al., "Sexually Active Teenagers are More Likely to be Depressed and to Attempt Suicide," The Heritage Foundation (June 3, 2003).

[13] National Longitudinal Survey of Adolescent Health, Wave II, 1996 Notes, Teenage boys aged 14-17.

[14] Hallfors, et al., "Which Comes First in Adolescence—Sex and Drugs or Depression?" *American Journal of Preventive Medicine* 29:3 (October 2005): 169.

[15] Hallfors, et al., 168; Hallfors, et al., "Adolescent Depression and Suicide Risk: Association with Sex and Drug Behavior," *American Journal of Preventive Medicine 27:3* (October 2004): 224-231; Martha W. Waller, et al., "Gender Differences in Associations Between Depressive Symptoms and Patterns of Substance Use and Risky Sexual Behavior among a Nationally Representative Sample of U.S. Adolescents," *Archives of Women's Mental Health 9:3* (May 2006): 139-150.

[16] *Love and Responsibility,* 136.

[17] Blessed John Paul II, *Letter to Families,* 14 (1994).

[18] "Adolescent Perceptions of Maternal Approval of Birth Control and Sexual Risk Behavior," *American Journal of Public Health,* October 2000).

[19] Centers for Disease Control, "Youth Risk Behavior Surveillance — United States, 2005" Morbidity and Mortality Weekly Report 55: SS-5 (June 9, 2006): 19.

[20] St. Bernard, Serm. XVIII in *Cantica.*

[21] *Love and Responsibility,* 134.

[22] Message of the Holy Father John Paul II to the Youth of the World on the Occasion of the XIX World Youth Day 2004, 22 February 2004.

[23] B.C. Miller, et al., "Dating Age and Stage as Correlates of Adolescent Sexual Attitudes and Behavior," *Journal of Adolescent Research* 1:3 (1986): 367.

[24] The National Center on Addiction and Substance Abuse, "National Survey of American Attitudes on Substance Abuse IX: Teen Dating Practices and Sexual Activity," Columbia University (August 2004), 6.

[25] The Australian Family Association 7:1 (February 2001). As reported by *Abstinence Network* 5:1 (Spring 2001): 9.

[26] John Paul II, January 26, 1999, Kiel Center, St. Louis, Missouri.

[27] Message of the Holy Father to the Youth of the World on the Occasion of the XV World Youth Day, June 29, 1999.